This Book Belongs To

~~~~~~~~~~~~~~~~~~~~~~~~~~
~~~~~~~~~~~~~~~~~~~~~~~~~~

Dedicated to Sydney & Thomas
from Grandad

Worlds Funniest A-Z Book of 737 Knock Knock Jokes

Pegasus Publishing

Who's There?
Worlds Funniest A-Z Book of 737 Knock Knock Jokes

Adapted by Tracy Rockwell

First Published in Australia in 2019
by Pegasus Publishing
PO Box 980, Edgecliff, NSW, 2027

Orders: pegasuspublishing@iinet.net.au
www.pegasuspublishing.com.au

All rights reserved. No part of this publication may be reproduced, stored in a retrieval system, or transmitted in any form or by any means, electronic, mechanical, photocopying, recording or otherwise, without the prior written permission of the copyright owner.

ISBN: 978-0-9942014-5-4

Copyright © Pegasus Publishing
An Ashnong Pty Ltd Company

Back Cover:
Funny Faces Collage

Contents

A....	6	N....	68
B....	15	O....	71
C....	21	P....	75
D....	27	Q....	78
E....	32	R....	80
F....	35	S....	83
G....	38	T....	88
H....	42	U....	92
I....	47	V....	94
J....	52	W....	96
K....	56	X....	101
L....	59	Y....	103
M....	63	Z....	106

Knock, knock!
Who's there?
Aardvark.
Aardvark who?
Aardvark a hundred miles for one of your smiles!

Knock! Knock!
Who's there?
A broken pencil.
A broken pencil who?
Never mind, it's pointless!

Knock, knock!
Who's there?
A herd.
A herd who?
A herd you were home, so I came over!

Knock, knock!
Who's there?
A little boy.
A little boy who?
A little boy who can't reach the doorbell.

Knock, knock!
Who's there?
A little girl.
A little girl who?
A little girl who's with the little boy!

Knock, knock!
Who's there?
A little old lady.
A little old lady who?
All this time, I had no idea you could yodel!

Knock! Knock!
Who's there?
A pile up.
A pile up who?
Ewwww!

Knock, knock!
Who's there?
Abba.
Abba who?
Abba'out turn! Quick march!

Knock, knock!
Who's there?
Abba.
Abba who?
Abba banana!

Knock, knock!
Who's there?
Abbie.
Abbie who?
Abbie birthday!

Knock, knock!
Who's there?
Abbot.
Abbot who?
Abbot you don't know who this is!

Knock, knock!
Who's there?
Abbott.
Abbott who?
Abbott time you open this door!

Knock, knock!
Who's there?
Abby.
Abby who?
Abby hive is where honey is made!

Knock, knock!
Who's there?
Abby.
Abby who?
Abby birthday to you!

Knock, knock!
Who's there?
Abby.
Abby who?
A bee just stung me!

Knock, knock!
Who's there?
Abby.
Abby who?
Abby C D E F G H...

Knock, knock!
Who's there?
Abyssinia.
Abyssinia who?
Abyssinia when I get back home!

Knock, knock!
Who's there?
Acid.
Acid who?
Acid back down and be quiet!

Knock, knock!
Who's there?
Acute.
Acute who?
Acute little boy!

Knock, knock!
Who's there?
Ada.
Ada who?
Ada burger for lunch!

Knock, knock!
Who's there?
Adair.
Adair who?
Adair once, but I'm bald now!

Knock, knock!
Who's there?
Adam.
Adam who?
Adam my way I'm coming through!

Knock, knock!
Who's there?
Adder.
Adder who?
Adder you get in here?

Knock, knock!
Who's there?
Adolph.
Adolph who?
Adolph ball hit me in the mouf... dat why I talk dis way!

Knock, knock!
Who's there?
Adore.
Adore who?
Adore is between us... open up!

Knock, knock!
Who's there?
Ahab.
Ahab who?
Ahab to go to the toilet now! Quick, open the door!

Knock, knock!
Who's there?
Ahmed.
Ahmed who?
Ahmed a mistake!

Knock, knock!
Who's there?
Aida.
Aida who?
Aida sandwich for lunch today!

Knock, knock!
Who's there?
Aitch.
Aitch who?
Do you need a tissue?

Knock, knock!
Who's there?
Al.
Al who?
Al give you a kiss if you open this door!

Knock, knock!
Who's there?
Alaska.
Alaska who?
Alaska one more time. Please let me in?

Knock, knock!
Who's there?
Alaska.
Alaska who?
Alaska no questions! You tella no lies!

Knock, knock!
Who's there?
Albert.
Albert who?
Albert you don't know who this is?

Knock, knock!
Who's there?
Alex.
Alex who?
Alex-plain later, just let me in!

Knock, knock!
Who's there?
Alex.
Alex who?
Alex the questions around here!

Knock, knock!
Who's there?
Alf.
Alf who?
Alf all if you don't catch me!

Knock, knock!
Who's there?
Alfie.
Alfie who?
Alfie terrible if you leave!

Knock, knock!
Who's there?
Alec.
Alec who?
Alec-tricity. Ain't that a shocker?

Knock, knock!
Who's there?
Alien.
Alien who?
Just how many aliens do you know?

Knock, knock!
Who's there?
Alison.
Allison who?
Alison to the radio?

Knock, knock!
Who's there?
Alota.
Alota who?
Alota good this is doing me!

Knock, knock!
Who's there?
Althea.
Althea who?
Althea later, alligator!

Knock, knock!
Who's there?
Alpaca.
Alpaca who?
Alpaca the trunk, you packa the suitcase!

Knock, knock!
Who's there?
Amanda.
Amanda who?
A man da fix your sink!

Knock, knock!
Who's there?
Amarillo.
Amarillo who?
Amarillo nice guy!

Knock, knock!
Who's there?
Amish.
Amish who?
You're not a shoe!

Knock, knock!
Who's there?
Amish.
Amish Who?
Awww... how sweet. I miss you too.

Knock, knock!
Who's there?
Amma.
Amma who?
Amma not going to tell you!

Knock, knock!
Who's there?
Ammonia.
Ammonia who?
Ammonia little girl who can't reach the doorbell!

Knock, knock!
Who's there?
Amos.
Amos who?
Amosquito just bit me!

Knock, knock!
Who's there?
Amy.
Amy who?
Amy fraid I've forgotten!

Knock, knock!
Who's there?
Andrew.
Andrew who?
Andrew a picture!

Knock, knock!
Who's there?
Anee.
Anee who?
Anee one you like!

Knock, knock!
Who's there?
Annie.
Annie who?
Annie body home?

Knock, knock!
Who's there?
Annie.
Annie who?
Annie way you can let me in?

Knock, knock!
Who's there?
Annie.
Annie who?
Annie way you can let me in... soon?

Knock, knock!
Who's there?
Annie.
Annie who?
Annie body going to open the door already?

Knock, knock!
Who's there?
Annie.
Annie who?
Annie thing you can do, I can do better.

Knock, knock!
Who's There?
Anita.
Anita who?
Anita to borrow a pencil!

Knock, knock!
Who's there?
Argo.
Argo who?
Argo down the shops if you aren't going to let me in!

Knock, knock!
Who's there?
Armageddon.
Armageddon who?
Armageddon out of here!

Knock, knock!
Who's there?
Army.
Army who?
Army and you still friends?

Knock, knock!
Who's there?
Apple.
Apple who? >
Knock, knock!
Who's there?
Apple.
Apple who? >
Knock, knock!
Who's there?
Apple!
Apple who? >
OK last one, knock, knock!!
Who's there?
Orange!
Orange who?
Orange you glad I didn't say Apple again?

Knock, knock!
Who's there?
Arncha.
Arncha who?
Arncha Going to let me in? It's freezing out here!

Knock, knock!
Who's there?
Art.
Art who?
Art ya gonna open the door for me?

Knock, knock!
Who's there?
Atch.
Atch who?
Bless you

Knock, knock!
Who's there?
Armageddon.
Armageddon who?
Armageddon a little bored. Let's go out.

Knock, knock!
Who's there?
Arthur.
Arthur who?
Arthur any more jellybeans in the jar?

Knock, knock!
Who's there?
Artichokes.
Artichokes who?
Artichokes when he eats too fast!

Knock, knock!
Who's there?
Atlas.
Atlas?
At... las it's the weekend!

Knock, knock!
Who's there?
Avenue.
Avenue who?
Avenue knocked on this door before?

Knock, knock!
Who's there?
Avery.
Avery who?
Avery time I come to your house we go through this!

Knock, knock!
Who's there?
Avon.
Avon who?
Avon you to open the door!

Knock, knock!
Who's there?
Avon.
Avon who?
Avon a box of cookies and a chocolate ice cream!

Knock, knock!
Who's there?
Avon.
Avon who?
Avon you to be my wife!

Knock, knock!
Who's there?
Ayatollah.
Ayatollah who?
Ayatollah you already!

Knock, knock!
Knock, knock!
Who's there !
B-4 !
B-4 who ?
B-4 I freeze to death, please open this door !

Knock, knock!
Who's there?
Bab.
Bab who?
Baboons are a type of Ape!

Knock, knock!
Who's there?
Back.
Back who?
Back off, I'm going to force my way in!

Knock, knock!
Who's there?
Bacon.
Bacon who?
Bacon a cake for your birthday!

Knock, knock
Who's there?
Banana.
Banana who?
Banana split!

Knock, knock!
Who's there?
Barbara.
Barbara who?
Barbara black sheep, have you any wool...

Knock, knock!
Who's There?
Barbie.
Barbie who?
Barbie Q Chicken!

Knock, knock!
Who's there?
Barry.
Barry who?
Barry the treasure where no one will find it!

Knock, knock!
Who's there?
Bart.
Bart who?
Bartween you and me, I'm sick of standing in the cold!

Knock, knock!
Who's there?
Bashful.
Bashful who who?
I'm too shy to tell you!

Knock, knock!
Who's there?
Bean.
Bean who?
Bean working too hard lately!

Knock, knock!
Who's there?
Bed.
Bed who?
Bed you can't guess who I am!

Knock, knock!
Who's there?
Bee.
Bee who?
Bee careful!

Knock, knock!
Who's there?
Beef.
Beef who?
Beefair now!

Knock, knock!
Who's there?
Beef.
Beef who?
Before I get mad, you'd better let me in!

Knock, knock!
Who's there?
Been.
Been who?
Been to any movies lately?

Knock, knock!
Who's there?
Beets.
Beets who?
Beets me!

Knock, knock!
Who's there?
Bella.
Bella who?
Bella bottom trousers!

Knock, knock!
Who's there?
Ben.
Ben who?
Ben down and look through the letter slot!

Knock, knock!
Who's there?
Ben.
Ben who?
Ben knocking on this door all morning, let me in!

Knock, knock!
Who's there?
Ben.
Ben who?
Ben a while since I last saw you!

Knock, knock!
Who's there?
Bernadette.
Bernadette who?
Bernadette my lunch! Now I'm starving!

Knock, knock!
Who's there?
Beth.
Beth Who?
Beth wisheth, thweetie!

Knock, knock!
Who's there?
Betty.
Betty who?
Betty late than never!

Knock, knock!
Who's there?
Betty.
Betty who?
Betty let me in or they'll be trouble!

Knock, knock!
Who's there?
Biafra.
Biafra who?
Biafra'id, be very afraid!

Knock, knock!
Who's there?
Bjorn.
Bjorn who?
Bjorn free!

Knock, knock!
Who's there?
Bless.
Bless who?
I didn't sneeze!

Knock, knock!
Who's there !
Bolivia !
Boliva who ?
Boliva me, I know what I'm talking about !

Knock, knock!
Who's there?
Bolton.
Bolton who?
Bolton the door! That's why I can't get in!

Knock, knock!
Who's there?
Boo.
Boo who?
Gosh, don't cry it's just a Knock, knock!joke.

Knock, knock!
Who's there
Boo.
Boo who?
I didn't mean to make you cry! It's just me!

Knock, knock!
Who's there?
Botany.
Botany who?
Botany good locks lately?

Knock, knock!
Who's there?
Boxer.
Boxer who?
Boxer tricks!

Knock, knock!
Who's there?
Brazil.
Brazil who?
Braz... il support a girls chest!

Knock, knock!
Who's there?
Britney Spears.
Britney Spears who?
Knock, knock - oops i did it again.

Knock, knock!
Who's there?
Broccoli.
Broccoli who?
Broccoli doesn't have a last name, silly.

Knock, knock!
Who's there?
Broken Pencil.
Broken Pencil who.
Never mind it's pointless!

Knock, knock!
Who's there?
Bruce.
Bruce who?
I Bruce easily, don't hit me !

Knock, knock!
Who's there?
Buddha.
Buddha who?
Buddha this slice of bread for me!

Knock, knock!
Who's there?
Burglar.
Burglar who?
Burglars don't knock!

Knock, knock!
Who's there?
Butch, Jimmy and Joe.
Butch, Jimmy and Joe who?
Butch your arms around me, Jimmy a little kiss and never let me Joe.

Knock, knock!
Who's there?
Butcher.
Butcher who?
Butcher arms around me!

Knock, knock!
Who's there?
Butcher.
Butcher who?
Butcher left leg in, Butcher left leg out...

Knock, knock!
Who's there?
Butcher.
Butcher who?
Butcher money where your mouth is!

Knock, knock!
Who's there?
Butter.
Butter who?
Butter be quick, I have to go to the bathroom!

Knock, knock!
Who's there?
Butter.
Butter who?
I butter not tell you!

Knock, knock!
Who's there !
Butter !
Butter who ?
Butter bring an umbrella, it looks like it might rain !

Knock, knock!
Who's there?
C-2.
C-2 who?
C-2 it that you remember me next time!

Knock, knock!
Who's there?
Caesar.
Caesar who?
Caesar quick, she's running away.

Knock, knock!
Who's there?
Caesar.
Caesar who?
Caesar a jolly good fellow!

Knock, knock!
Who's there?
CD.
CD who?
CD guy on your doorstep?

Knock, knock!
Who's there?
Cameron.
Cameron who?
Cameron film are what you need to take pictures!

Knock, knock!
Who's there?
Candice.
Candice who?
Candice door open, please?

Knock, knock!
Who's there?
Canoe.
Canoe who?
Canoe help me with my work?

Knock, knock!
Who's there?
Canoe.
Canoe who?
Canoe come out or what?

Knock, knock!
Who's there?
Cargo.
Cargo who?
No, car go "beep beep"!

Knock, knock!
Who's there?
Carl.
Carl who?
Carload of furniture for you... where do you want it?

Knock, knock!
Who's there?
Carlotta.
Carlotta who?
Carlotta trouble when it breaks down!

Knock, knock!
Who's there?
Carmen.
Carmen who?
Carmen let me in already!

Knock, knock!
Who's there?
Carmen.
Carmen who?
Carmen get it!

Knock, knock!
Who's there?
Carrie.
Carrie who?
Carrie on with what you're doing!

Knock, knock!
Who's there?
Carrie.
Carrie who?
Carrie me inside, I'm tired!

Knock, knock!
Who's there?
Cash.
Cash who?
I didn't realize you were some kind of nut!

Knock, knock!
Who's there?
Cash.
Cash who?
No thanks, I'll have some peanuts.

Knock, knock!
Who's there?
Cash.
Cash who?
Yes! I've always known you were a bit nutty!

Knock, knock!
Who's there?
Caterpillar.
Caterpillar who?
Cat-er-pillar of feline society!

Knock, knock!
Who's there?
Cattle.
Cattle who?
Cattle always purr when you pet it!

Knock, knock!
Who's there?
Cecil.
Cecil who?
Cecil have music wherever she goes!

Knock, knock!
Who's there?
Celeste.
Celeste who?
Celeste time I come around here!

Knock, knock!
Who's there?
Celia.
Celia who?
Celia later alligator!

Knock, knock!
Who's there?
Cereal.
Cereal who?
Cereal pleasure to meet you!

Knock, knock!
Who's there?
Cheese.
Cheese who?
Cheese a jolly good fellow!

Knock, knock!
Who's there?
Cheese .
Cheese who?
Cheese a nice girl.

Knock, knock!
Who's there?
Chick!
Chick who?
Chick your oven, I can smell burning!

Knock, knock!
Who's there?
Chicken.
Chicken who?
Chicken your pocket... my keys are missing!

Knock, knock!
Who's there?
Claire.
Claire who?
Claire the snow from your path or someone will have an accident!

Knock, knock!
Who's there?
Claire.
Claire who?
Claire the way, I'm coming through!

Knock, knock!
Who's there?
Closure.
Closure who?
Closure mouth when you're eating!

Knock, knock!
Who's there?
Colin.
Colin who?
Colin all cars! Colin all cars!

Knock, knock!
Who's there?
Cologne.
Cologne who?
Cologne me names wont get you anywhere!

Knock, knock!
Who's there?
Control freak.
Co...
You should say "Control freak who" now.

Knock, knock!
Who's there?
Cow-go.
Cow-go who?
Cow go MOO!

Knock, knock!
Who's there?
Cows go.
Cow's go who?
No, silly. Cows go Moo!

Knock, knock!
Who's there?
Cow says.
Cow says who?
No, a cow says mooooo!

Knock, knock!
Who's there?
Cook.
Cook who?
Yes you are!

Knock, knock!
Who's there?
Comb.
Comb who?
Comb on down and I'll tell you!

Knock, knock!
Who's there?
Cornflakes.
Cornflakes who?
I'll tell you tomorrow, it's a cereal!

Knock, knock!
Who's there?
Cosi.
Cosi who?
Cosi had to!

Knock, knock!
Who's there?
Cousin!
Cousin who?
Cousin stead of opening the door, you're making me stand here!

Knock, knock!
Who's there?
Crispin.
Crispin who?
Crispin juicy is how I like my chicken!

Knock, knock!
Who's there?
Cupid!
Cupid who?
Cupid quiet in there.

Knock, knock!
Who's there?
Curry.
Curry who?
Curry me back home please!

Knock, knock!
Who's there?
Custer.
Custer who?
Custer a penny to find out!

Knock, knock!
Who's there?
Cymbals.
Cymbals wh?
Cymbals have horns and others don't!

Knock, knock!
Who's there?
Cynthia.
Cynthia who?
Cynthia you been away I missed you!

Knock, knock!
Who's there?
Czech.
Czech who?
Czech before you open the door!

Knock, knock!
Who's there?
D-1.
D-1 who?
D-1 who knocked!

Knock, knock!
Who's there?
Dad.
Dad who?
Dad fuel to the fire!

Knock, knock!
Who's there?
Dad.
Dad who?
Dad 2 and 2 to get 4!

Knock, knock!
Who's there?
Daisy.
Daisy who?
Daisy me rollin, are over!

Knock, knock!
Who's there?
Dale.
Dale who?
Dale come if you ask dem!

Knock, knock!
Who's there?
Dan.
Dan who?
Dan druff!

Knock, knock!
Who's there?
Dancer.
Dancer who?
Dancer is simple, it's me!

Knock, knock!
Who's there?
Danielle.
Danielle who?
Danielle so loud... I can hear you!

Knock, knock!
Who's there?
Daryl.
Daryl who?
Saryl never be another you!

Knock, knock!
Who's there?
Dat.
Dat who?
Dat's all folks!

Knock, knock!
Who's there?
Data.
Data who?
Data remember!

Knock, knock!
Who's there?
Datsun.
Datsun who?
Datsun old joke!

Knock, knock!
Who's there?
Dave.
Dave who?
Dave-andalised our house!

Knock, knock!
Who's there?
Debate.
Debate who?
Debate goes on de hook if you want to catch de fish!

Knock, knock!
Who's there?
Debbie.
Debbie who?
Debbie or not to be!

Knock, knock!
Who's there?
Déja.
Déja who?
Knock, knock!

Knock, knock!
Who's there?
Denise.
Denise who?
Denise are between the waist and the feet!

Knock, knock!
Who's there?
Des.
Des who?
Des no bell! Dat's why I'm knocking!

Knock, knock!
Who's there?
Despair.
Despair who?
Despair tyre is flat!

Knock, knock!
Who's There?
Dewey.
Dewey who?
Dewey have to use a condom every time?

Knock, knock!
Who's there?
Diesel.
Diesel who?
Diesel help with your cold! Take two every four hours!

Knock, knock!
Who's there?
Disguise.
Disguise who?
Disguise crazy!

Knock, knock!
Who's there?
Dish.
Dish who?
Dish is a nice place!

Knock, knock!
Who's there?
Dishes.
Dishes who?
Dishes a very bad joke!

Knock, knock!
Who's there?
Dishes.
Dishes who?
Dishes the Police... come out with your hands up!

Knock, knock!
Who's there?
Dishes.
Dishes who?
Dishes a nice place you got here!

Knock, knock!
Who's there?
Diss.
Diss who?
Diss is ridiculous! Let me in!

Knock, knock!
Who's there?
Doctor.
Doctor who?
Thats right!

Knock, knock!
Who's there?
Don.
Don who?
Don just stand there... open the door!

Knock, knock!
Who's there?
Doris.
Doris who?
Doris locked. Open up!

Knock, knock!
Who's there?
Doris.
Doris who?
The Doris locked, why do you think I'm knocking?

Knock, knock!
Who's there?
Double.
Double who?
W!

Knock, knock!
Who's there?
Doughnut.
Doughnut who?
Doughnut ask, its a secret!

Knock, knock!
Who's there?
Dozen.
Dozen who?
Dozen all this knocking bother you already?

Knock, knock!
Who's there?
Dozen.
Dozen who?
Dozen anyone want to let me in?

Knock, knock!
Who's there?
Duncan.
Duncan who?
Duncan disorderly!

Knock, knock!
Who's there?
Dunnip.
Dunnip who?
Errgh have u... please use the toilet next time!

Knock, knock!
Who's there?
Dwayne.
Dwayne who?
Dwayne the bathtub, I'm drowning!

Knock, knock!
Who's there?
Dynamite.
Dynamite who?
Dyna... mite, if you ask her nicely!

Knock, knock!
Who's there?
Earl.
Earl who?
Earl be glad to get to bed, I'm tired.

Knock, knock!
Who's there?
Ears.
Ears who?
Ears another Knock, knock! joke for you!

Knock, knock!
Who's there?
Egbert.
Egbert who?
Egbert no bacon please!

Knock, knock!
Who's there?
Egg.
Egg who?
Eggstremely disappointed you still don't recognize me.

Knock, knock!
Who's there?
Egg.
Egg who?
Eggcited to see me?

Knock, knock!
Who's there?
Effie.
Effie who?
Effie'd known you were coming... he'd have stayed home!

Knock, knock!
Who's there?
Eliza.
Eliza who?
Eliza awake at night thinking about you!

Knock, knock!
Who's there?
Ella.
Ella who?
Ella-mentary, my dear fellow!

Knock, knock!
Who's there?
Ellie.
Ellie who?
Ellie-phants never forget!

Knock, knock!
Who's there?
Ellis.
Ellis who?
Ellis between K and M!

Knock, knock!
Who's there?
Elsie.
Elsie who?
Elsie you down at the park!

Knock, knock!
Who's there?
Emma.
Emma who?
Emma bit cold out here, can you let me in?

Knock, knock!
Who's there?
Empty.
Empty who?
Empty - V (MTV)

Knock, knock!
Who's there?
Etch.
Etch who?
Bless you, friend.

Knock, knock!
Who's there?
Euripides.
Euripides who?
Euripides jeans, you pay for them!

Knock, knock!
Who's there?
Euripides.
Euripides who?
Euripides pants... then you Eumenides pants!

Knock, knock!
Who's there?
Europe.
Europe who?
Europe early this morning!

Knock, knock!
Who's there?
Europe.
Europe who?
No I'm not!

Knock, knock!
Who's there?
Evan.
Evan who?
Evan you should know who I am!

Knock, knock!
Who's there?
F-2.
F-2 who?
F-2 go to the bathroom!

Knock, knock!
Who's there?
Fangs.
Fangs who?
Fangs for letting me in!

Knock, knock!
Who's there?
Fanny.
Fanny who?
Fanny the way you keep asking... 'who's there?'

Knock, knock!
Who's there?
Fantasy.
Fantasy who?
Fantasy a walk on the beach?

Knock, knock!
Who's there?
Felix.
Felix who?
Felix my ice cream... I'm going to lick his!

Knock, knock!
Who's there?
Ferdie.
Ferdie who?
Ferdie last time open this door!

Knock, knock!
Who's there?
Felix.
Felix who?
Felix my lolly, I'll whack him.

Knock, knock!
Who's there?
Fiddle.
Fiddle?
Fiddle make you happy I'll tell you!

Knock, knock!
Who's there?
Figs.
Figs who?
Figs the doorbell, it's broken!

Knock, knock!
Who's there?
Flea.
Flea who?
Flea blind mice!

Knock, knock!
Who's there?
Fork.
Fork who?
Fork-get it, I'm leaving!

Knock, knock!
Who's there?
Fossil.
Fossil who?
Fossil last time, open the door!

Knock, knock!
Who's there?
Foster.
Foster who?
Foster than a speeding bullet!

Knock, knock!
Who's there?
Fozzie.
Fozzie who?
Fozzie hundredth time... my name is Nick!

Knock, knock!
Who's there?
France.
France who?
France of the family!

Knock, knock!
Who's there?
Francis.
Francis who?
Francis the home of the Eiffel Tower!

Knock, knock!
Who's there?
Freeze.
Freeze who?
Freeze a jolly good fellow!

Knock, knock!
Who's there?
Frank.
Frank who?
Frank you for being my friend!

Knock, knock!
Who's there?
Fry.
Fry who?
Fryday is the end of the week!

Knock, knock!
Who's there?
Gala.
Gala who?
Galafornia here I come!

Knock, knock!
Who's there?
Gandhi.
Gandhi who?
Gandhi come out and play?

Knock, knock!
Who's there?
Garden.
Garden who?
Garden the treasure, it's precious!

Knock, knock!
Who's there?
Gary.
Gary who?
Gary on smiling!

Knock, knock!
Who's there?
Gay.
Gay who?
Gay Topen, that's how the cows got out!

Knock, knock!
Who's there?
Genoa.
Genoa who?
Ge...noa good place to have a meal around here?

Knock, knock!
Who's there?
Genoa.
Genoa who?
Genoa any new Knock, knock! jokes?

Knock, knock!
Who's there?
Geoff.
Geoff who?
Geoff feel like a drink!

Knock, knock!
Who's there?
George.
George who?
George-us lady, give me a kiss!

Knock, knock!
Who's there?
Gerald.
Gerald who?
It's Ger...ald friend from school!

Knock, knock!
Who's there?
German border patrol.
German border patrol who?
Ve vill ask ze questions!

Knock, knock!
Who's there?
Gino.
Gino who?
Gino me... now open the door!

Knock, knock!
Who's there?
Giuseppe.
Giuseppe who?
Giuseppe da credit cards!

Knock, knock!
Who's there?
Gizza.
Gizza who?
Gizza kiss!

Knock, knock!
Who's there?
Gladys.
Gladys who?
Gladys Friday, finally the weekend starts!

Knock, knock!
Who's there?
Gladys.
Gladys who?
Gladys Saturday aren't you?

Knock, knock!
Who's there?
Goat.
Goat who?
Goat to the door and find out.

Knock, knock!
Who's there?
Godiva.
Godiva who?
Godiva terrible headache, do you have an aspirin?

Knock, knock!
Who's there?
Goliath.
Goliath who?
Goliath down, thou looketh tired!

Knock, knock!
Who's there?
Goose.
Goose who?
Goose who's knocking at your door again!

Knock, knock!
Who's there?
Gopher.
Gopher who?
Go for help, I've been tied up!

Knock, knock!
Who's there?
Gorilla.
Gorilla who?
Gorilla burger! I've got the buns!

Knock, knock!
Who's there?
Grammar.
Grammar who?
Grammar is in the Old People's Home!

Knock, knock!
Who's there?
Grant.
Grant who?
Grant you three wishes!

Knock, knock!
Who's there?
Grub.
Grub who?
Grub hold of my hand and lets go!

Knock, knock!
Who's there?
Gudonov.
Gudonov who?
Gudonov to eat!

Knock, knock!
Who's there?
Guinea.
Guinea who?
Guinea some money so I can buy some food!

Knock, knock!
Who's there?
Gus.
Gus who?
No, you guess who... I already know!

Knock, knock!
Who's there?
Guthrie.
Guthrie who?
Guthrie Musketeers!

Knock, knock!
Who's there?
H.
H who?
Bless you!

Knock, knock!
Who's there?
Hacienda.
Hacienda who?
Haci... enda the story! It's bedtime now!

Knock, knock!
Who's there?
Hada.
Hada who?
Had a great time, how about you?

Knock, knock!
Who's there?
Haden.
Haden who?
Haden seek!

Knock, knock!
Who's there?
Haifa.
Haifa who?
Haifa cake is better than none!

Knock, knock!
Who's there?
Hair.
Hair who?
Hair today, gone tomorrow!

Knock, knock!
Who's there?
Hair.
Hair who?
I'm hair to stay!

Knock, knock!
Who's there?
Haitit.
Haitit who?
Haitit when you talk like that!

Knock, knock!
Who's there?
Hammond.
Hammond who?
Hammond eggs!

Knock, knock!
Who's there?
Hand.
Hand who?
Handover your money!

Knock, knock!
Who's there?
Hanna.
Hanna who?
Hanna partridge in a pear tree!

Knock, knock!
Who's there?
Hans.
Hans who?
Hans are on the end of your arms!

Knock, knock!
Who's there?
Hans.
Hans who?
Hans off the table!

Knock, knock!
Who's there?
Harlow.
Harlow who?
Harlow will you go!

Knock, knock!
Who's there?
Harmony.
Harmony who?
Harmony electricians does it take to change a lightbulb?

Knock, knock!
Who's there?
Harry.
Harry who?
Harry up and answer this door!

Knock, knock!
Who's there?
Harry.
Harry who?
Harry up and let me in!

Knock, knock!
Who's there?
Harry.
Harry who?
Harry up, it's cold out here!

Knock, knock!
Who's there?
Hatch.
Hatch who?
Bless you and please cover your mouth next time.

Knock, knock!
Who's there?
Havalock.
Havalock who?
Havalock put on your door!

Knock, knock!
Who's there?
Hawaii.
Hawaii who?
I'm fine. Hawaii you?

Knock, knock!
Who's there?
Heaven.
Heaven who?
Heaven seen you for a long time.

Knock, knock!
Who's there?
Heidi.
Heidi who?
Heidi 'cided to come over to play!

Knock, knock!
Who's there?
Heidi.
Heidi who?
Heidi ho!

Knock, knock!
Who's there?
Hello.
Hello who?
Hello dolly!

Knock, knock!
Who's there?
Hester.
Hester who?
Hester la vista... baby!

Knock, knock!
Who's there?
Hey.
Hey who?
Hey who, hey who... its off to work we goo!

Knock, knock!
Who's there?
Hijack.
Hijack who?
Hi Jack... where's Jill?

Knock, knock!
Who's there?
Hip.
Hip who?
Hippopotamus.

Knock, knock!
Who's there?
Hockey.
Hockey who?
Hockey doesn't work, so I had to knock!

Knock, knock!
Who's there?
Honey bee.
Honey bee who?
Honey bee a dear and open up, would you?

Knock, knock!
Who's there?
Hoo.
Hoo who?
Are you a owl?

Knock, knock!
Who's there?
House.
House who?
House you doing?

Knock, knock!
Who's there?
Howard.
Howard who?
Howard you like to be knocking for a change?

Knock, knock!
Who's there?
Howard.
Howard who?
Howard you like a big kiss?

Knock, knock!
Who's there?
Howard.
Howard who?
Howard I know?

Knock, knock!
Who's there?
Howl.
Howl who?
Howl you know it's really me unless you open the door?

Knock, knock!
Who's there?
Hugo.
Hugo who?
Hugo the high road, and I'll go the low road!

Knock, knock!
Who's there?
Huron.
Huron who?
Huron time for once!

Knock, knock!
Who's there?
I did up.
I did up who?
Ha ha you did a poo!

Knock, knock!
Who's there?
I eat mop.
I eat mop who?
That's revolting.

Knock, knock!
Who's there?
I eat mop.
I eat mop who?
Dammit, man, that is way too much information!

Knock, knock!
Who's there?
I scream.
I scream who?
I scream tastes good on a hot day!

Knock, knock!
Who's there?
I smell mop.
I smell mop who?
Ew.

Knock, knock!
Who's there?
Ice cream.
Ice cream who?
Ice cream if you don't let me in!

Knock, knock!
Who's there?
Icing.
Icing who?
Icing so loud, the neighbors can hear!

Knock, knock!
Who's there?
Icon.
Icon who?
Icon tell you another Knock, knock! joke... Do you want me to?

Knock, knock!
Who's there?
Icy.
Icy who?
I see your underwear!

Knock, knock!
Who's there?
Icy.
Icy who?
You see me, do you need glasses or something?

Knock, knock!
Who's there?
Ida.
Ida who?
Ida hard time getting here!

Knock, knock!
Who's there?
Ida.
Ida who?
Ida know why I love you like I do!

Knock, knock!
Who's there?
Ike.
Ike who?
Ike could have danced all night!

Knock, knock!
Who's there?
Knock, knock!
Who's there?
Knock, knock!
Who's there?
Knock, knock!
For the last time who's there?
I'm sorry, but mum told me never speak to strangers!

Knock, knock!
Who's there?
Ima.
Ima who?
Ima going home if you don'ta let me in!

Knock, knock!
Who's there?
Ima.
Ima who?
Ima catchin da cold out here... let me in!

Knock, knock!
Who's there?
Ima.
Ima who?
Ima psychiatrist. I'm here 'cause you won't open up!

Knock, knock!
Who's there?
Ines.
Ines who?
Ines second I'm going to turn around and go home!

Knock, knock!
Who's there?
Interrupting cow!
Interr...
MOOOO!!

Knock, knock!
Who's there?
Interrupting doctor.
Interr...
You've got cancer.

Knock, knock!
Who's there?
Interrupting Pirate.
Interr...
ARRRR!!

Knock, knock!
Who's there?
Interrupting Raven.
Interr...
CAAWW!!!

Knock, knock!
Who's there?
Iona.
Iona who?
Iona new car!

Knock, knock!
Who's there?
Ira.
Ira who?
Ira-te if you don't let me in!

Knock, knock!
Who's there?
Iran.
Iran who?
Iran all the way here. Let me in already!

Knock, knock!
Who's there?
Iran.
Iran who?
Iran over here to tell you this!

Knock, knock!
Who's there?
Irish.
Irish who?
Irish you a nice day.

Knock, knock!
Who's there?
Irish.
Irish who?
Irish you a Merry Christmas!

Knock, knock!
Who's there?
Irish.
Irish who?
Irish I had a million dollars!

Knock, knock!
Who's there?
Irish.
Irish who?
Irish I knew some more Knock, knock! jokes!

Knock, knock!
Who's there?
Irish stew.
Irish stew who?
Irish stew in the name of the law!

Knock, knock!
Who's there?
Is your name.
Is your name who?
No... my name is _____!

Knock, knock!
Who's there?
Isabelle.
Isabelle who?
Is a bell working?

Knock, knock!
Who's there?
Isabelle.
Isabelle who?
Isabelle working, or should I keep knocking?

Knock, Knock.
Who's there?
Island.
Island who?
Island here and you won't open up!

Knock, knock!
Who's there?
Iva.
Iva who?
I've a sore hand from knocking!

Knock, knock!
Who's there?
Ivan.
Ivan who?
No...Ivanhoe!

Knock, knock!
Who's there?
Ivor.
Ivor who?
Ivor you let me in or I'll break the door down!

Knock, knock!
Who's there?
Ivor.
Ivor who?
Ivor you let me in or I'll climb through the window.

Knock, knock!
Who's there?
Jack.
Jack who?
Jack your egos at the door!

Knock, knock!
Who's there?
Jackson.
Jackson who?
Jackson the telephone, you'd better answer it!

Knock, knock!
Who's there?
Jacqueline.
Jacqueline who?
Jacqueline and Hyde!

Knock, knock!
Who's there?
Jacques.
Jacques who?
Jacques of all trades!

Knock, knock!
Who's there?
Jam.
Jam who?
Jam mind, I'm trying to get in!

Knock, knock!
Who's there?
Jamaica.
Jamaica who?
Jamaica mistake? Just let me in!

Knock, knock!
Who's there?
Jamaica.
Jamaica who?
Jamaica mistake?

Knock, knock!
Who's there?
Janet.
Janet who?
Janet has too many holes in it, the fish will escape!

Knock, knock!
Who's there?
Japan.
Japan who?
Japan is too hot, ouch!

Knock, knock!
Who's there?
Java.
Java who?
Java dog in your house, I hear one barking!

Knock, knock!
Who's there?
Java.
Java who?
Java dollar you can lend me?

Knock, knock!
Who's there?
Jaws.
Jaws who?
Jaws truly!

Knock, knock!
Who's there?
Jean.
Jean who?
Jeanius...ask me anything?

Knock, knock!
Who's there?
Jeff.
Jeff who?
Jeff in one ear, can you speak louder?

Knock, knock!
Who's there?
Jerry.
Jerry who?
Jerry funny, let me in!

Knock, knock!
Who's there?
Jess.
Jess who?
Jess me and my shadow!

Knock, knock!
Who's there?
Jess.
Jess who?
Jess let me in.

Knock, knock!
Who's there?
Jester.
Jester who?
Jester silly old man!

Knock, knock!
Who's there?
Jester.
Jester who?
Jester minute... I'm looking for my keys!

Knock, knock!
Who's there?
Jethro.
Jethro who?
Je... thro a rope out the window!

Knock, knock!
Who's there?
Jewell.
Jewell who?
Jewell know me when you see me!

Knock, knock!
Who's there?
Jilly.
Jilly who?
Jilly out here, so let me in!

Knock, knock!
Who's there?
Jim.
Jim who?
Jim mind if I come in?

Knock, knock!
Who's there?
Joe.
Joe who?
Joe away, I'm not talking to you.

Knock, knock!
Who's there?
Juan.
Juan who?
Juan two three o'clock, four o'clock rock!

Knock, knock!
Who's there?
Justice.
Justice who?
Justice I thought... you wont let me in!

Knock, knock
Who's there?
Justin.
Justin who?
Just in the neighborhood, thought I would drop by.

Knock, knock!
Who's there?
Justin.
Justin who?
Justin time to give you a hug.

Knock, knock!
Who's there?
Justin.
Justin who?
Justin time for dinner.

Knock, knock!
Who's there?
K-2.
K-2 who?
K-2 come in!

Knock, knock!
Who's there?
Kanga.
Kanga who?
Actually, it's kangaroo!

Knock, knock!
Who's there?
Kareem.
Kareem who?
Kareem of the crop!

Knock, knock!
Who's there?
Keanu.
Keanu who?
Keanu let me in, it's cold out here!

Knock, knock!
Who's there?
Keith.
Keith who?
Keith me, my thweet preenth!

Knock, knock!
Who's there?
Ken.
Ken who?
Ken I come in?

Knock, knock!
Who's there?
Ken.
Ken who?
Ken you let me in?

Knock, knock!
Who's there?
Kent.
Kent who?
Kent you tell? I'm standing right here!

Knock, knock!
Who's there?
Kentucky.
Kentucky who?
Kentucky too well, have a sore throat!

Knock, knock!
Who's there?
Kenya.
Kenya who?
Kenya guess who is it?

Knock, knock!
Who's there?
Kenya.
Kenya who?
Kenya keep the noise down... Im trying to sleep!

Knock, knock!
Who's there?
Kermit.
Kermit who?
Kermit a crime and you'll get locked up!

Knock, knock!
Who's there?
Ketchup.
Ketchup who?
Ketchup with me and I'll tell you!

Knock, knock!
Who's there?
Kermit.
Kermit who?
Kermit a crime and you'll get locked up!

Knock, knock!
Who's there?
King Tut.
King Tut who?
King Tut-key fried chicken!

Knock, knock!
Who's there?
Kipper.
Kipper who?
Kipper you hands offa me!

Knock, knock!
Who's there?
Kitten.
Kitten who?
Kitt... en the park hit me with a stick!

Knock, knock!
Who's there?
Kiwi.
Kiwi who?
Kiwi go to the store?

Knock, knock!
Who's there?
Kyoto.
Kyoto who?
Kyoto jail, do not pass go, do not collect $200!

Knock, knock!
Who's there?
Larva.
Larva who?
I larva you!

Knock, knock!
Who's there?
Larva.
Larva who?
Larva cup of coffee!

Knock, knock!
Who's there?
Lass.
Lass who?
Are you a cowboy?

Knock, knock!
Who's there?
Laura.
Laura who?
Are you a Laura biding citizen?

Knock, knock!
Who's there?
Lauren.
Lauren who?
Lauren order!

Knock, knock!
Who's there?
Leaf.
Leaf who?
Leaf me alone!

Knock, knock!
Who's there?
Lee.
Lee who?
Lee me alone - I've got a headache!

Knock, knock!
Who's there?
Lee King.
Lee King who?
Leeking bucket!

Knock, knock!
Who's there?
Lego.
Lego who?
Lego of me and I'll tell you!

Knock, knock!
Who's there?
Leif.
Leif who?
Leif me alone!

Knock, knock!
Who's there?
Len.
Len who?
Len me some money?

Knock, knock!
Who's there?
Leonie.
Leonie who?
Leonie here... all by myself!

Knock, knock!
Who's there?
Les.
Les who?
Les go out for dinner!

Knock, knock!
Who's there?
Les.
Les who?
Les go for a swim!

Knock, knock!
Who's there?
Letter.
Letter who?
Letter in or she'll knock the door down!

Knock, knock!
Who's there?
Lettuce.
Lettuce who?
Lettuce in, it's cold out here!

Knock, knock!
Who's there?
Lieder.
Lieder who?
Lieder of the pack!

Knock, knock!
Who's there?
Lillian.
Lillian who?
Lillian the garden!

Knock, knock!
Who's there?
Lion.
Lion who?
Lion down is the best thing to do when you're sick!

Knock, knock!
Who's there?
Lion.
Lion who?
Lion on your doorstep, open up!

Knock, knock!
Who's there?
Lisa.
Lisa who?
I want to Lisa new car!

Knock, knock!
Who's there?
Lionel.
Lionel who?
Lionel roar if you don't feed him!

Knock, knock!
Who's there?
Loaf.
Loaf who?
I don't just like bread, I loaf it.

Knock, knock!
Who's there?
Lock.
Lock who?
Lock who it is, after all this time!

Knock, knock!
Who's there?
Lois.
Lois who?
Lois the opposite of high!

Knock, knock!
Who's there?
Lucinda.
Lucinda who?
Luci... nda sky with diamonds!

Knock, knock!
Who's there?
Lucy.
Lucy who?
Lucy...lastic can be embarrassing!

Knock, knock!
Who's There?
Lucy.
Lucy, who?
Loose elastic and stinky undies!

Knock, knock!
Who's there?
Luke.
Luke who?
Luke through the the peep hole and find out.

Knock, knock!
Who's there?
Mabel.
Mabel who?
Mabel doesn't work either!

Knock, knock!
Who's there?
Madam.
Madam who?
Ma..dam foot got stuck in the door!

Knock, knock!
Who's there?
Mae.
Mae who?
Mae be I'll tell you or Mae be I won't!

Knock, knock!
Who's there?
Maggot.
Maggot who?
Mag... got me these new jeans today!

Knock, knock!
Who's there?
Maia.
Maia who?
Maia aunt and uncle are coming to stay!

Knock, knock!
Who's there?
Major.
Major who?
Major day with this joke, haven't I?

Knock, knock!
Who's there?
Major.
Major who?
Major B. Hindsor when you got spanked!

Knock, knock!
Who's there?
Major.
Major who?
Major answer didn't I!

Knock, knock!
Who's there?
Mandy.
Mandy who?
Mandy life boats... we're sinking!

Knock, knock!
Who's there?
Mango.
Mango who?
Mango to the door and just answer it!

Knock, knock!
Who's there?
Manny.
Manny who?
Manny try, but few are chosen!

Knock, knock!
Who's there?
Manuel.
Manuel who?
Man... uel be sorry if you don't open this door!

Knock, knock!
Who's there?
Marie.
Marie who?
Marie the one you love!

Knock, knock!
Who's there?
Marietta.
Marietta who?
Mari... etta whole cake!

Knock, knock!
Who's there?
Markus.
Markus who?
Markus down for two tickets will you!

Knock, knock!
Who's there?
Marmalade.
Marmalade who?
Marmalade me... said the little chicken!

Knock, knock!
Who's there?
Mary.
Mary who?
Mary me?

Knock, knock!
Who's there?
Mary.
Mary who?
Mary Christmas and a happy new year!

Knock, knock!
Who's there?
Mary Lee.
Mary Lee who?
Mary Lee down the stream.

Knock, knock!
Who's there?
Max.
Max who?
Max no difference. Open the door!

Knock, knock!
Who's there?
Maybelle.
Maybelle who?
Maybelle doesn't ring either!

Knock, knock!
Who's there?
Mayonnaise.
Mayonnaise who?
Mayonnaise are sore from reading too many Knock, knock! jokes!

Knock, knock!
Who's there?
Mecca.
Mecca who?
You Mecca me happy!

Knock, knock!
Who's there?
Meg.
Meg who?
Meg up your mind - Let me in!

Knock, knock!
Who's there?
Mess.
Mess who?
You messed with the wrong door my friend!

Knock, knock!
Who's there?
Mickey.
Mickey who?
Mickey is stuck in the lock!

Knock, knock!
Who's there?
Midas.
Midas who?
Midas well let me in!

Knock, knock!
Who's there?
Mike Snifferpippets.
Mike Snifferpippets who?
Oh come on... how many Mike Snifferpippets' do you know? Now let me in, it's cold out here!

Knock, knock!
Who's there?
Mikey.
Mikey who?
Mikey doesn't fit in the keyhole.

Knock, knock!
Who's there?
Mikey.
Mikey who?
Mikey doesn't work so help me out, would you?

Knock, knock!
Who's there?
Milky.
Milky who?
Baby want milky!

Knock, knock!
Who's there?
Miniature.
Miniature who?
Miniature let me in... I'll tell ya!

Knock, knock!
Who's there?
Minnie.
Minnie who?
Minnie people are waiting out here!

Knock, knock!
Who's there?
Mister.
Mister who?
Mister last bus home.

Knock, knock!
Who's there?
Moppet.
Moppet who?
Moppet up before someone slips!

Knock, knock!
Who's there?
Mortimer.
Mortimer who?
Mortimer than meets the eyes!

Knock, knock!
Who's there?
Moustache.
Moustache who?
I moustache you a question, but I can shave it for tomorrow.

Knock, knock!
Who's there?
My panther.
My panther who?
My panther falling down!

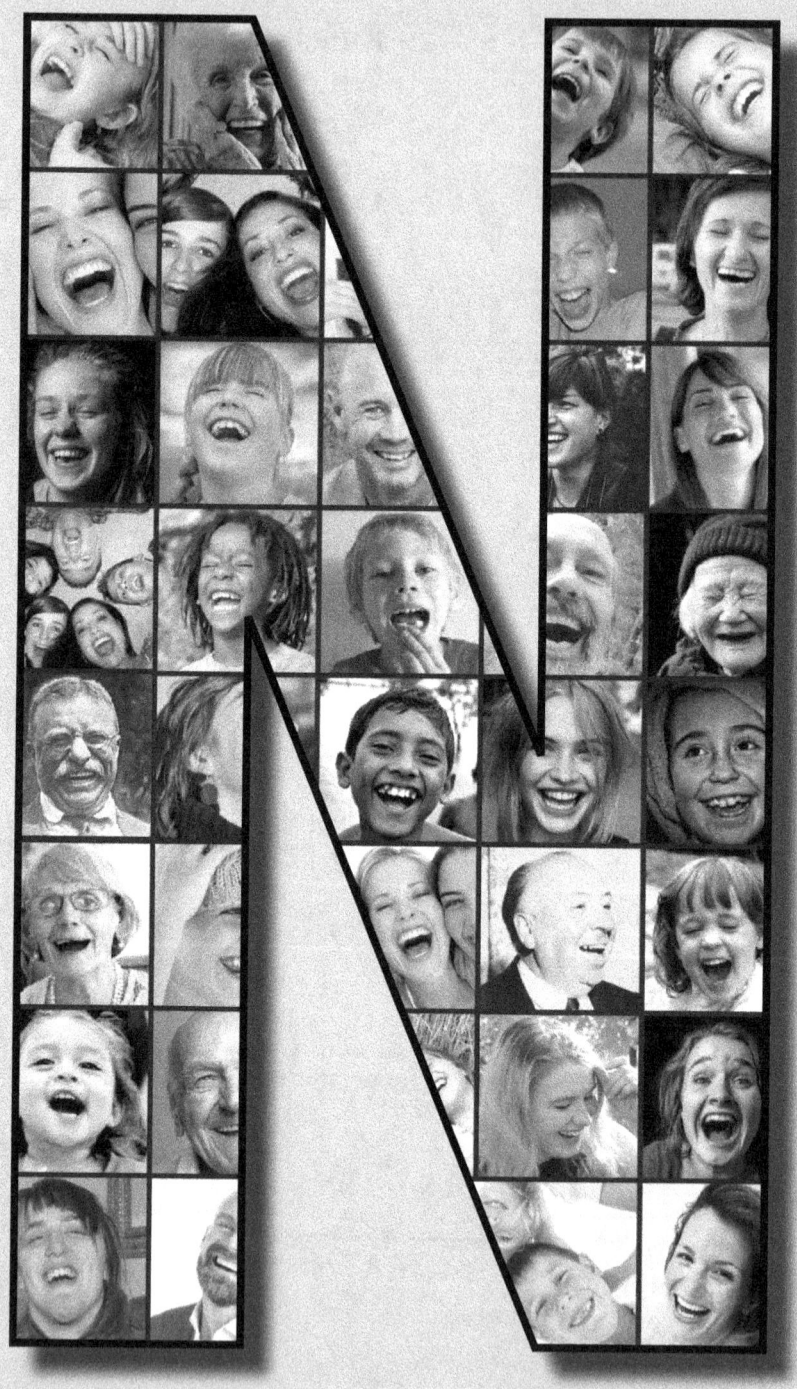

Knock, knock!
Who's there?
Nadya.
Nadya who?
Nadya head if you understand what I'm saying!

Knock, knock!
Who's there?
Nanna.
Nanna who?
Nanna your business, that's who.

Knock, knock!
Who's there?
Needle.
Needle who?
Needle little help gettin' through.

Knock, knock!
Who's there?
Needle.
Needle who?
Needle little money for the movies.

Knock, knock!
Who's there?
Neil.
Neil who?
Neil down and take a peek!

Knock, knock!
Who's there?
Nettie.
Nettie who?
Nettie as a fruitcake!

Knock, knock!
Who's there?
Noah.
Noah who?
Noah good place for a meal?

Knock, knock!
Who's there?
Noah.
Noah who?
Noah counting for taste!

Knock, knock!
Who's there?
Noah.
Noah who?
Noah yes? What's your decision?

Knock, knock!
Who's there?
Noah.
Noah who?
Noah way to open the door?

Knock, knock!
Who's there?
Noah.
Noah who?
Noah good place we can get something to eat?

Knock, knock!
Who's there?
Nobel.
Nobel who?
No bell, that's why I knocked!

Knock, knock!
Who's there?
Nobody.
Nobody who?
No...body, just a skeleton!

Knock, knock!
Who's there?
Noise.
Noise who?
Noise to see you!

Knock, knock!
Who's there?
Norma Lee.
Norma Lee who?
Norma Lee I'd be at school, but Ive got the day off!

Knock, knock!
Who's there?
Norway.
Norway who?
There's Norway I'm leaving until you open this door!

Knock, knock!
Who's there?
Nose.
Nose who?
I nose plenty more Knock, knock! jokes!

Knock, knock!
Who's there?
Nunya.
Nunya who?
Nunya business!

Knock, knock!
Who's there?
Nurse.
Nurse who?
Nur... sense talking to you!

Knock, knock!
Who's there?
Obi Wan.
Obi Wan who?
Obi Wan of the good guys!

Knock, knock!
Who's there?
Offer.
Offer who?
Offer gotten who I am!

Knock, knock!
Who's there?
Ocelot.
Ocelot who?
Ocelot of questions, don't you?

Knock, knock!
Who's there?
Odysseus.
Odysseus who?
Odysseus the last straw!

Knock, knock!
Who's there?
Offenbach.
Offenbach who?
Offenbach is performed!

Knock, knock!
Who's there?
Ogre.
Ogre who?
Ogre take a flying leap!

Knock, knock!
Who's there?
Ogre.
Ogre who?
Ogre the hill and far away!

Knock, knock!
Who's there?
Oily.
Oily who?
The Oily bird catches the worm!

Knock, knock!
Who's there?
Olive.
Olive who?
Olive in the house across the street!

Knock, knock!
Who's there?
Olive.
Olive who?
O live you.

Knock, knock!
Who's there?
Olive.
Olive who?
Olive right next door to you.

Knock, knock!
Who's there?
Olive.
Olive who?
Olive you. Do you love me too?

Knock, knock!
Who's there?
Olivia.
Olivia who?
O... liv... ia , open up!!!

Knock, knock!
Who's there?
Onya.
Onya who?
Onya mark, get set... GO!

Knock, knock!
Who's there?
Ooze.
Ooze who?
Ooze in charge around here?

Knock, knock!
Who's there?
Opportunity.
Opportunity who?
Opportunity doesn't knock twice!

Knock, knock!
Who's there?
Orange.
Orange who?
Orange you glad I stopped by?

Knock, knock!
Who's there?
Orange.
Orange who?
Orange you going to answer the door?

Knock, knock!
Who's there?
Orange.
Orange who?
Orange you sick of these knock-knock jokes?

Knock, knock!
Who's there?
Orange.
Orange who?
Orange you going to let me in?

Knock, knock!
Who's there?
Omar.
Omar who?
Omar goodness, wrong door!

Knock, knock!
Who's there?
Omelet.
Omelet who?
Omelet'in you kiss me!

Knock, knock!
Who's there?
Orson.
Orson who?
Orson cart!

Knock, knock!
Who's there?
Oscar.
Oscar who?
Oscar silly question... get a silly answer!

Knock, knock!
Who's there?
Oswald.
Oswald who?
Oswald my bubble gum!

Knock, knock!
Who's there?
Otto.
Otto who?
Otto know... I've got amnesia!

Knock, knock!
Who's there?
Owl.
Owl who?
Owl be sad if you don't let me in!

Knock, knock!
Who's there?
Owls say.
Owls say who?
Yep!

Knock, knock!
Who's there?
Ozzie.
Ozzie who?
Ozzie you later!

Knock, knock!
Who's there?
Panther.
Panther who?
Panther no panth, I'm going thwimming!

Knock, knock!
Who's there?
Parish.
Parish who?
Parish is the capitol of France!

Knock, knock!
Who's there?
Passion.
Passion who?
Just Passion by and thought I'd pop in!

Knock, knock!
Who's there?
Pasta.
Pasta who?
Pasta salt please!

Knock, knock!
Who's there?
Pasture.
Pasture who?
Pasture bedtime... isn't it?

Knock, knock!
Who's there?
Peas.
Peas who?
Peas pass the butter!

Knock! Knock!
Who's there?
Pecan.
Pecan who?
Pecan somebody your own size!

Knock, knock!
Who's there?
Pencil.
Pencil who?
Your pencil fall down if you don't wear a belt!

Knock, knock!
Who's there?
Percy.
Percy who?
Percy vere and you'll go a long way!

Knock, knock!
Who's there?
Philip.
Philip who?
Philip my cup, I'm thirsty!

Knock, knock!
Who's there?
Philip.
Philip who?
Philip up my glass please, I'm thirsty!

Knock, knock!
Who's there?
Phone.
Phone who?
Phonely I'd known it was you!

Knock, knock!
Who's there?
Phony.
Phony who?
Phony you'd told me the truth!

Knock, knock!
Who's there?
Phyllis.
Phyllis who?
Phyllis a glass of water... please?

Knock, knock!
Who's there?
Police.
Police who?
Police (please) may I come in?

Knock, knock!
Who's there?
Police.
Police who?
Police hurry up, it's chilly outside!

Knock, knock!
Who's there?
Police.
Police who?
Police stop telling these awful Knock, knock! jokes!

Knock, knock
Who's there?
Poll.
Poll who?
Police!

Knock, knock!
Who's there?
Poop.
Poop who?
Please use the upstairs toilet!

Knock, knock!
Who's there?
Pudding.
Pudding who?
Pudding on your shoes before your trousers is a bad idea!

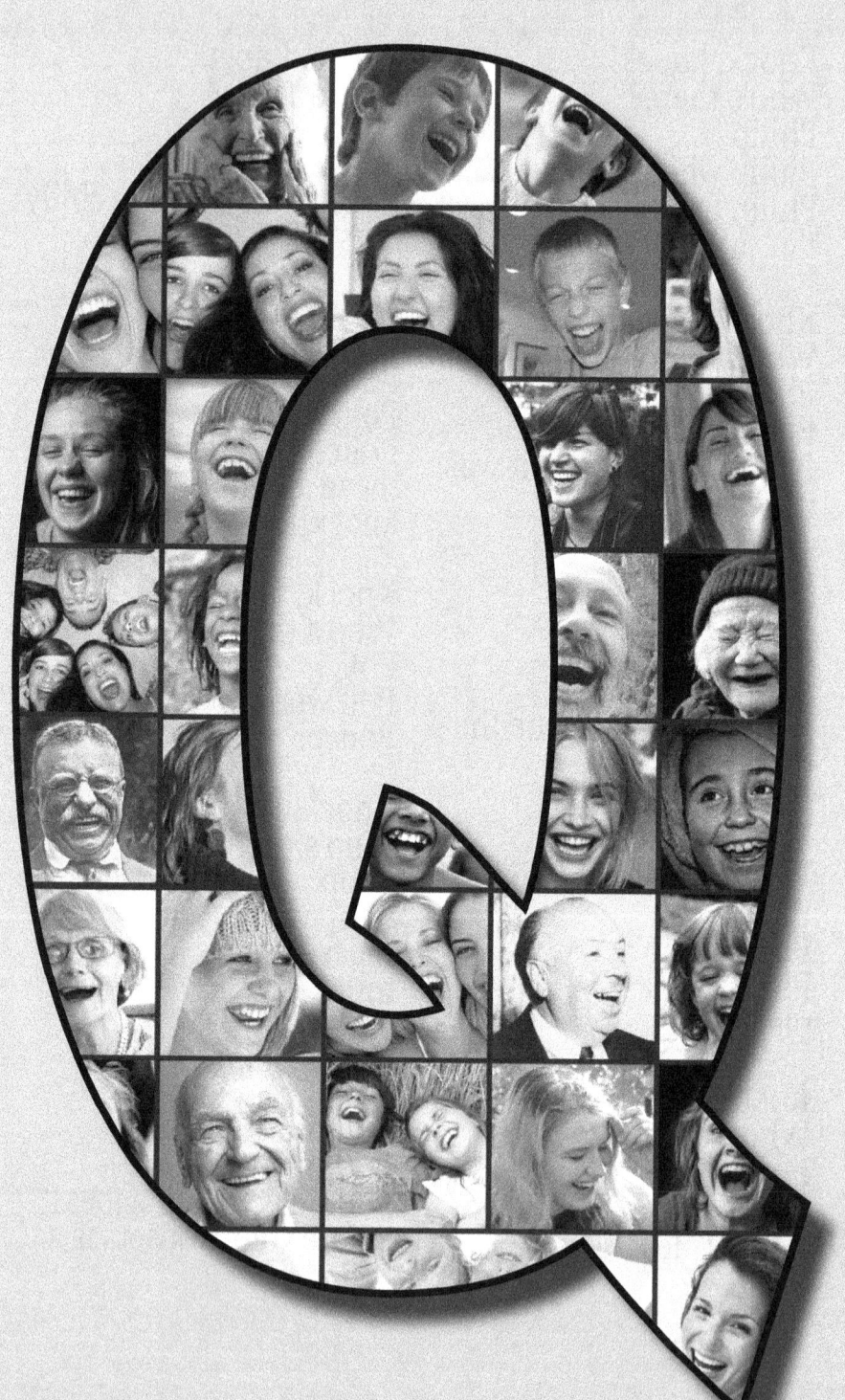

Knock, knock!
Who's there?
Quacker.
Quacker who?
Quacker another bad joke and I'm leaving!

Knock, knock!
Who's there?
Quacker.
Quacker who?
Do you have a quacker for my parrot?

Knock, knock!
Who's there?
Quebec.
Quebec who?
Quebec to the end of the line!

Knock, knock!
Who's there?
Queen.
Queen who?
Queen as a whistle!

Knock, knock!
Who's there?
Quentin.
Quentin who?
Quentin my thirst!

Knock, knock.
Who's there?
Quiet Tina.
Quiet Tina who?
Quiet Tina library!

Knock, knock!
Who's there?
Quiet Tina.
Quiet Tina who?
Quiet Tina courtroom... the monkey wants to speak!

Knock, knock!
Who's there?
Quincy.
Quincy who?
You Quincy the doctor now!

Knock, knock!
Who's there?
Rabbit.
Rabbit who?
Rabbit carefully, it's fragile!

Knock, knock!
Who's there?
Radio.
Radio who?
Radio not, here I come!

Knock, knock!
Who's there?
Raoul.
Raoul who?
You have to Raoul with the punches!

Knock, knock!
Who's there?
Ray.
Ray who?
Ray-member me?!

Knock, knock!
Who's there?
Razor.
Razor who?
Razor hands and dance the boogie!

Knock, knock!
Who's there?
Razor.
Razor who?
Razor hands, this is a stick up!

Knock, knock!
Who's there?
Reed.
Reed who?
Reed-turn to sender!

Knock, knock!
Who's there?
Renata.
Renata who?
I Renata milk... can you spare some?

Knock, knock!
Who's there?
Riot.
Riot who?
Riot on time here I am.

Knock, knock!
Who's there?
Rhoda.
Rhoda who?
Row, row, Roda boat!

Knock, knock!
Who's there?
Roach.
Roach who?
Roach you a letter, but I didn't send it!

Knock, knock!
Who's there?
Robin.
Robin who?
No.. Robin Hood!

Knock, knock!
Who's there?
Robin.
Robin who?
Robin you, now hand over the cash.

Knock, knock!
Who's there?
Robin.
Robin who?
Robin your house!

Knock, knock!
Who's there?
Robin.
Robin who?
Robin the piggy bank again.

Knock, knock!
Who's there?
Roach.
Roach who?
Roach you a letter, did you get it?

Knock, knock!
Who's there?
Rose.
Rose who?
Rose early to come see you1

Knock, knock!
Who's there?
Rough.
Rough who?
Rough, rough, rough! It's your dog!

Knock, knock!
Who's there?
Roxanne.
Roxanne who?
Roxanne pebbles are all over my garden!

Knock, knock!
Who's there?
Russell.
Russell who?
Russell up something to eat, I'm starving!

You ask your friends...
"Say... Knock, knock!"
They say... Knock, knock!
You say... Who's there?
Then... sit back and watch their expression? It's priceless!

Knock, knock!
Who's there?
Sacha.
Sacha who?
Sacha lot of questions!

Knock, knock!
Who's there?
Sadie.
Sadie who?
Sadie air is hot out here!

Knock, knock!
Who's there?
Sadie.
Sadie who?
Sadie magic words and I'll tell you!

Knock, knock!
Who's there?
Sancho.
Sancho who?
Sancho a letter, but you never answered!

Knock, knock!
Who's there?
Sal.
Sal who?
Sal-long, long way to Tipperary!

Knock, knock!
Who's there?
Samantha.
Samantha who?
Sam...antha others have already gone!

Knock, knock!
Who's there?
Sarah.
Sarah who?
Sarah nother way in?

Knock, knock!
Who's there?
Sarah.
Sarah who?
Sa-rah phone I could use?

Knock, knock!
Who's there?
Sari.
Sari who?
Sari I took so long!

Knock, knock!
Who's there?
Sawyer.
Sawyer who?
Sawyer lights on and thought I'd drop by!

Knock, knock!
Who's there?
Says.
Says who?
Says me, that's who?

Knock! Knock!
Who's there?
Scold.
Scold who?
Scold outside... let me in!

Knock, knock!
Who's there?
Scott.
Scott who?
Scott nothing to do with you!

Knock, knock!
Who's there?
Shamp.
Shamp who?
Why... do I have head lice?

Knock, knock!
Who's there?
Shelby.
Shelby who?
Shelby comin' round the mountain when she comes!

Knock, knock!
Who's there?
Sherlock.
Sherlock who?
Sherlock your door shut tight.

Knock, knock!
Who's there?
Sherwood.
Sherwood who?
Sure would like you to open the door!

Knock, knock!
Who's there?
Sherwood.
Sherwood who?
Sherwood love to come inside! It's cold out here!

Knock, knock!
Who's there?
Shirley.
Shirley who?
Shirley you know by now!

Knock, knock!
Who's there?
Shocking.
Shocking who?
Shocking you!

Knock, knock!
Who's there?
Sister.
Sister who?
Sister right place... or am I lost?

Knock, knock!
Who's there?
Smell mop.
Smell mop who?
Eww, no thanks. I don't want to smell your poo!

Knock, knock!
Who's there?
Snow.
Snow who?
Snowbody!

Knock, knock!
Who's there?
Snow.
Snow who?
Snow use. I forgot my name again!

Knock, knock!
Who's there?
Snow.
Snow who?
Snow use askin' when you can just open.

Knock, knock!
Who's there?
Snow.
Snow who?
Snow good asking me!

Knock, knock!
Who's there?
Some.
Some who?
Some day you'll recognize me, hopefully.

Knock, knock!
Who's there?
Somebody.
Somebody who?
Somebody too short to ring the doorbell!

Knock, knock!
Who's there?
Sorry.
Sorry who?
Sorry wrong door!

Knock, knock!
Who's there?
Spell.
Spell who?
W-H-O

Knock, knock!
Who's there?
Spell.
Spell who?
Okay, okay: W.H.O.

Knock, knock!
Who's there?
Stan.
Stan who?
Stan back or I'll shoot!

Knock, knock!
Who's there?
Stopwatch.
Stopwatch who?
Stopwatch you're doing and pay attention!

Knock, knock!
Who's there?
Stopwatch.
Stopwatch who?
Stopwatch you're doing and open this door!

Knock, knock!
Who's there?
Stopwatch.
Stopwatch who?
Stopwatcha doin' and open the stupid door.

Knock, knock!
Who's there?
Stupid.
Stupid who?
Stupid you, that's who.

Knock, knock!
Who's there?
Sultan.
Sultan who?
Sultan pepper!

Knock, knock!
Who's there?
Suspense.
Suspense who?
...

Knock, knock!
Who's there?
Tad.
Tad who?
Tad's all folks!

Knock, knock!
Who's there?
Tailor.
Tailor who?
Tailor head... your call !

Knock, knock!
Who's there?
Tamara.
Tamara who?
Tamara is another day!

Knock, knock!
Who's there?
Tank.
Tank who?
You're welcome!

Knock, knock!
Who's there?
Telly.
Telly who?
Telly your friend to come out!

Knock, knock!
Who's there?
Ten.
Ten who?
Ten to your own business!

Knock, knock!
Who's there?
Tennis.
Tennis who?
Tennis is five plus five!

Knock, knock!
Who's there?
Tex.
Tex who?
Tex two to Tango!

Knock, knock!
Who's there?
Theodore.
Theodore who?
Theodore wasn't open so I knocked!

Knock, knock!
Who's there?
Theodore.
Theodore who?
Theodore got slammed on my finger!

Knock, knock!
Who's there?
Theresa.
Theresa who?
Theresa are very green!

Knock, knock!
Who's there?
Theresa.
Theresa who?
Theresa are really big here!

Knock, knock!
Who's there?
Thermos.
Thermos who?
Thermos be a better Knock, knock! joke than this!

Knock, knock!
Who's there?
Thermos.
Thermos who?
Thermos be a better way to get through to you.

Knock, knock!
Who's there?
Thistle.
Thistle who?
Thistle be the last time I'll knock!

Knock, knock!
Who's there?
Thor.
Thor who?
Thor knuckles from knocking!

Knock, knock!
Who's there?
Tibet.
Tibet who?
Early Tibet, makes early to rise!

Knock, knock!
Who's there?
Tim.
Tim who?
Tim you got scared!

Knock, knock!
Who's there?
A titch.
A titch who?
Bless you!

Knock, knock!
Who's there?
To.
To who?
No, to whom.

Knock, knock!
Who's there?
Toby.
Toby who?
Toby or not to be... that is the question!

Knock! Knock!
Who's there?
Too Na.
Too Na who?
Too Na Fish!

Knock, knock!
Who's there?
Tooth.
Tooth who?
Tooth or dare!

Knock, knock!
Who's there?
Troy.
Troy who?
Troy the bell instead!

Knock, knock!
Who's there?
Troy.
Troy who?
Troy as I may, I can't reach the bell!

Knock, knock!
Who's there?
Turnip.
Turnip who?
Turnip the volume. I love this song.

Knock, knock!
Who's there?
Turnip.
Turnip who?
Turnip for school tomorrow, or you're in big trouble!

Knock, knock!
Who's there?
Twit.
Twit who?
Did anyone else hear an owl?

Knock, knock!
Who's there?
Tyrone.
Tyrone who?
Tyrone shoelaces!

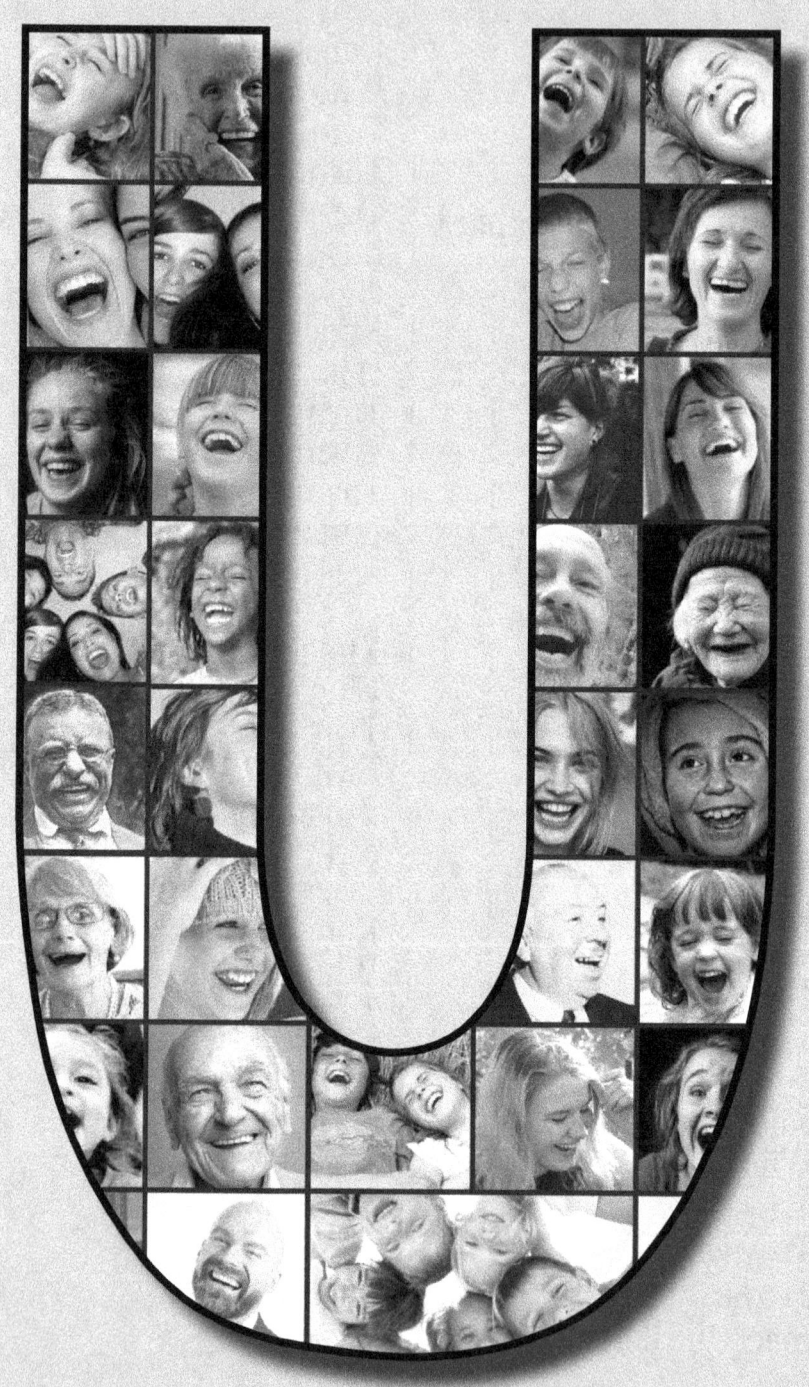

Knock, knock!
Who's there?
U.
U who?
U for me, and me for U!

Knock, knock!
Who's there?
U-2.
U-2 who?
U-2 can buy a brand-new car for only $199 a month!

Knock, knock!
Who's there?
U-4.
U-4 who?
U-4 me and me for you!

Knock, knock!
Who's there?
U-8.
U-8 who?
U-8 my lunch!

Knock, knock!
Who's there?
UCI.
UCI who?
UCI had to knock because your doorbell didn't work!

Knock, knock!
Who's there?
Udder.
Udder who?
Udder madness are these Knock, knock!jokes!

Knock, knock!
Who's there?
Una.
Una who?
No I don't... tell me!

Knock, knock!
Who's there?
Urine.
Urine who?
Urine trouble if you don't open the door.

Knock, knock
Who's there?
Utah.
Utah who?
Utah one who told me to knock!

Knock, knock!
Who's there?
Value.
Value who?
Value be my valentine?

Knock, knock!
Who's there?
Vanda.
Vanda who?
Vanda you vant me to come around?

Knock, knock!
Who's there?
Vault.
Vault who?
Vault...sing Matilda, vaultsing Matilda!

Knock, knock!
Who's there?
Venice.
Venice who?
Ven...ice your mother coming home?

Knock, knock!
Who's there?
Venice.
Venice who?
Ven...ice this door gonna open?

Knock, knock!
Who's there?
Venice.
Venice who?
Ven...ice your doorbell going to be fixed?

Knock, knock!
Who's there?
Vera.
Vera who?
Vera all the flowers gone?

Knock, knock!
Who's there?
Voodoo.
Voodoo who?
Voodoo you think you are!

Knock, knock!
Who's there?
Voodoo.
Voodoo who?
Voodoo you think you are, asking me so many questions?

Knock, knock!
Who's there?
Waddle.
Waddle who?
Waddle you give me to leave you alone?

Knock, knock!
Who's there?
Wade.
Wade who?
Wade up little Susie!

Knock, knock!
Who's there?
Wafer.
Wafer who?
I been Wafer long time, but I'm back now!

Knock, knock!
Who's there?
Wah.
Wah who?
Well... you don't have to get so excited about it!

Knock, knock!
Who's there?
Waiter.
Waiter who?
Waiter I get my hands on you!

Knock, knock!
Who's there?
Waiter.
Waiter who?
Waiter minute, while I tie my shoe!

Knock, knock!
Who's there?
Wanda.
Wanda who?
Wanda buy some cookies?

Knock, knock!
Who's there?
Water.
Water who?
Water you doing? Open the door!

Knock, knock!
Who's there?
Water.
Water who?
Water way to answer the door!

Knock, knock!
Who's there?
Water.
Water who?
Water you doing? Just open the door!

Knock, knock!
Who's there?
Water.
Water who?
Water friends for!

Knock, knock!
Who's there?
Watson.
Watson who?
Watson TV tonight?

Knock, knock?
Who's there?
Wayne.
Wayne who?
Wayne drops are falling on my head!

Knock, knock?
Who's there?
Wayne.
Wayne who?
Wayne, wayne go away... come again another day!

Knock, knock!
Who's there?
Weaken.
Weaken who?
Weaken work it out, don't worry!

Knock, knock!
Who's there?
Weed.
Weed who?
Weed better mow the lawn before it gets too long!

Knock, knock!
Who's there?
Weevil.
Weevil who?
Weevil rock you.

Knock, knock!
Who's there?
Weirdo.
Weirdo who?
Weirdo you think you're going?

Knock, knock!
Who's there?
Wenceslas.
Wenceslas who?
Wenceslas bus home?

Knock, knock!
Who's there?
Wendy.
Wendy who?
Wendy bell works again I won't have to knock anymore..

Knock, knock!
Who's there?
Who.
Who who?
Is there an owl in here?

Knock, knock!
Who's there?
Who.
Who who?
Wait... I can hear an echo!

Knock, knock!
Who's there?
Wicked.
Wicked who?
Wicked be a great couple if you just gave me a chance!

Knock, knock!
Who's there?
Will.
Will who?
Will you let me in?

Will you remember me in a day? ... a week? ... a month? ... a year?... they say 'Yes'!
Knock, knock!
Who's there?
See... you forgot me already!

Knock, knock!
Who's there?
Will.
Will who?
Will you let me in? It's freezing out here!

Knock, knock!
Who's there?
Will.
Will who?
Will you just open the door already?

Knock, knock!
Who's there?
William.
William who?
Willia...mind your own business!

Knock, knock!
Who's there?
Wilma.
Wilma who?
Wilma dinner be ready soon?

Knock, knock!
Who's there?
Winner.
Winner who?
Winner you gonna get this door fixed?

Knock, knock!
Who's there?
Wire.
Wire who?
Wire you always asking me, who's there?

Knock, knock!
Who's there?
Witches.
Witches who?
Witches the way home?

Knock, knock!
Who's there?
Wooden shoe.
Wooden shoe who?
Wooden shoe like to know!

Knock, knock!
Who's there?
Wooden shoe.
Wooden shoe who?
Wooden shoe like to hear another joke?

Knock, knock!
Who's there?
Woodward.
Woodward who?
Woodward have come, but he was busy!

Knock, knock!
Who's there?
Wool.
Wool who?
Wool you get me a drink?

Knock, knock!
Who's there?
Woody.
Woody who?
Woody you want!

Knock, knock!
Who's there?
Wurlitzer.
Wurlitzer who?
Wurlitzer one for the money, two for the show...

Knock, knock!
Who's there?
Wyn.
Wyn who?
Wyn or lose, its the taking part that counts!

Knock, knock!
Who's there?
X.
X who?
Are you having X for breakfast!

Knock, knock!
Who's there?
X.
X who?
X-tremely pleased to meet you!!

Knock, knock!
Who's there?
Xavier.
Xavier who?
Xavier your money for a rainy day!

Knock, knock!
Who's there?
Xavier.
Xavier who?
Xavier your breath... I'm not leaving!

Knock, knock!
Who's there?
Xena.
Xena who?
Xena minute!

Knock, knock!
Who's there?
Xenia.
Xenia who?
Xenia stealing my candy!

Knock, knock!
Who's there?
Ya.
Ya who?
Wow. You sure are excited to see me!

Knock, knock!
Who's there?
Ya.
Ya who?
I'm excited to see you too!

Knock, knock!
Who's there?
Ya.
Ya who?
Yahoo! I'm just as psyched to see you!

Knock, knock!
Who's there?
Ya.
Ya who?
Well, no thanks, I'm more of a Google person.

Knock, knock!
Who's there?
Ya.
Ya who?
Ride-em cowboy!

Knock, knock!
Who's there?
Yacht.
Yacht who?
Yacht to know me by now!

Knock, knock!
Who's there?
Yam.
Yam who?
Yam what I am!

Knock, knock!
Who's there?
Yee.
Yee who?
What? Are you a cowboy?

Knock, knock!
Who's there?
Yehuda.
Yehuda who?
Yehuda dance all night!

Knock, knock!
Who's there?
Yelp.
Yelp who?
Yelp me, my nose is stuck in the keyhole!

Knock, knock!
Who's there?
Yellow.
Yellow who?
Yellow-ver the noise, I can hardly hear you!

Knock, knock!
Who's there?
Yoda.
Yoda who?
Yoh da boss.

Knock, knock!
Who's there?
York.
York who?
York coming over to my place!

Knock, knock
Who's there?
You forgot me already!

Knock, knock!
Who's there?
You.
You who?
Did you call?

Knock, knock!
Who's there?
Your mother.
Your mother who?
My mother has a key!

Knock, knock!
Who's there?
Yugo.
Yugo who?
Yugo first, I'm right behind you!

Knock, knock!
Who's there?
Yukon.
Yukon who?
Yukon say that again!

Knock, knock!
Who's there?
Yul.
Yul who?
Yul never guess!

Knock, knock!
Who's there?
Yvonne.
Yvonne who?
Yvonne to be alone?

Knock, knock!
Who's there?
Zac.
Zac who?
Zac of candy in my pocket.

Knock, knock!
Who's there?
Zaiden.
Zaiden who?
Zaiden is were zai-bear lives.

Knock, knock!
Who's there?
Zany.
Zany who?
Zany body home?

Knock, knock!
Who's there?
Zeb.
Zeb who?
Zeb been any mail delivered for me?

Knock, knock!
Who's there?
Zeke.
Zeke who?
Zeke and you shall find!

Knock, knock!
Who's there?
Zesty.
Zesty who?
Zesty home of Mister Smith?

Knock, knock!
Who's there?
Zombies.
Zombies who?
Zombies make honey, and zombies just fly around!

Knock, knock!
Who's there?
Zoom.
Zoom who?
Zoom did you expect!

**Knock, knock!
Who's there?
Zax.
Zax who?
Zax all folks!**

www.ingramcontent.com/pod-product-compliance
Lightning Source LLC
Chambersburg PA
CBHW050439010526
44118CB00013B/1605